JONESTOWN &
other madness

Also by Pat Parker:

Child of Myself
Pit Stop
Womanslaughter
Movement in Black

JONESTOWN &
other madness

poetry by pat parker

Firebrand
Books
Ithaca, New York 14850

Book design by Allison Platt
Cover design by Cassandra Maxwell-Simmons and Betsy Bayley
Typesetting by Tracy Hammer

Library of Congress Cataloging in Publication Data
Parker, Pat, 1944 -
  Jonestown & other madness
    Contents: Love isn't—Bar conversation—My brother
    —[etc.]
    I. Title.
PS3566.lt6847J6 1985   811'.54   85-1679
ISBN 0-932379-01-X
ISBN 0-932379-00-1 (pbk.)

foreword

This book came about because we have become too quiet. We go to our jobs and raise our families and turn our minds away from the madness that surrounds us.

The tragedy of Jonestown occurred in 1978. It is amazing to me that we have not demanded better explanations of what happened. As I travel and talk with people, I find that most of them do not believe what they have been told. Yet we still know very little. I must ask the question: If 900 white people had gone to a country with a Black minister and 'committed suicide,' would we have accepted the answers we were given so easily?

I find it difficult to accept the answers of Jonestown. I find it equally difficult in the case of Priscilla Jones, or to realize that in 1984, straight people remain sufficiently terrified by the gay lifestyle that a gay rights bill protecting against job discrimination needs to be 'studied' by the governor of California.

Most of all, it is frightening to me that we live with the madness, that we continue to move through our lives as if these—and more—were normal occurrences. We are a nation in great trouble. It is time for those with vision to speak out loudly before the madness consumes us all.

Pat Parker
March 10, 1984
Oakland, California

contents

love isn't

I wish I could be
the lover you want
come joyful
bear brightness
like summer sun

Instead
I come cloudy
bring pregnant women
with no money
bring angry comrades
with no shelter

I wish I could take you
run over beaches
lay you in sand
and make love to you

Instead
I come rage
bring city streets
with wine and blood
bring cops and guns
with dead bodies and prison

I wish I could take you
travel to new lives
kiss ninos on tourist buses
sip tequila at sunrise

Instead
I come sad
bring lesbians
without lovers
bring sick folk
without doctors
bring children
without families

I wish I could be
your warmth
your blanket

All I can give
is my love.

I care for you
I care for our world
if I stop
caring about one
it would be only
a matter of time
before I stop
loving
the other.

bar conversation

Three women were arrested for
assault recently after they beat
up a woman who put a swastika
on another woman's shoulder during
a S & M encounter.

It's something you should write about.
If you talk about it
then women will listen
and know it's ok.
Now, envision one poet sitting in a bar
not cruising
observing the interactions
and then sitting face to face
with a young woman
who wants a spokesperson for
sado-masochism
among lesbians.
The first impulse is to dismiss
the entire conversation as more
ramblings of a *SWG*

(read Silly White Girl:
derogatory
characterization
used by minorities for
certain members of the
caucasian race.)

The second is to run rapidly
in another direction.
Polite poets do not run,
throw up, or strike
the other person in a conversation.
What we do is let our minds ramble.

So nodding in the appropriate places
I left the bar
traveled
first to the sixties
back to the cramped living rooms
activist dykes
consciousness-raising sessions
I polled the women there
one by one
Is this what it was all about?
Did we brave the wrath of threatened bar owners
so women could wear handkerchiefs in their pockets?
One by one I asked.
Their faces faded
furrows of frowns on their brows.
I went to the halls
where we sat hours upon hours
arguing with Gay men
trying to build a united movement
I polled the people there
one by one

Is this why we did it?
Did we grapple with our own who hated us
so women could use whips and chains?
The faces faded
puzzled faces drift out of vision.
I returned to the jails
where women sat bruised and beaten
singing songs of liberation
through puffed lips
I polled the women there
one by one
Is this why we did it?
Did we take to the streets
so women can carve swastikas on their bodies?

Hundreds and hundreds of women
pass by
no, march by
chant, sing, cry
I return to the voice
the young voice in the bar
and I am angry
the vision of women playing
as Nazis, policemen, rapists
taunts me
mocks me
words drift through

it's always by consent
we are oppressed by other dykes
who don't understand
and I am back in the bar
furious
the poll is complete
no, no no no
this is not why we did it
this is not why we continue to do.

We need not play at being victim
we need not practice pain
we need not encourage helplessness
they lurk outside our doors
follow us through the streets
and claim our lives daily.
We must not offer haven
for fascists and pigs
be it real or fantasy
the line is too unclear.

my brother

for Blackberri

I

It is a simple ritual.
Phone rings
Berri's voice
low, husky
'What's you're doing?'
'Not a thing,
you coming over?'
'Well, I thought I'd
come by.'
A simple ritual.
He comes
we eat
watch television
play cards
play video games
some nights
he sleeps over
others
he goes home
sometimes
he brings a friend
more often
he doesn't.
A simple ritual.

II

It's a pause that alerts me
tells me this time
is hard time
the pain has risen
to the water line
we rarely verbalize
there is no need.

Within this lifestyle
there is much to undo you.

Hey look at the faggot!
When I was a child
our paper boy was Claude
every day
seven days a week
he bared the Texas weather
the rain that never stopped
walked through the Black section
where sidewalks had not
yet been invented
and ditches filled with water.
Walk careful Claude
across the plank
that served as sidewalk
sometime tips into the murky water

or heat
wet heat
that covers your pores
cascades rivulets of
stinging sweat down your body.
Our paper boy Claude
bared the weather well
each day he came
and each Saturday at dusk
he would come to collect.

My parents liked Claude.
Each Saturday Claude polite
would come
always said thank you
whether we had the money
or not.
Each Saturday
my father would say
Claude is a nice boy
works hard
goes to church
gives his money to his mother
and each Sunday
we would go to church
and there would be Claude
in his choir robes
til the Sunday
when he didn't come.

Hey look at the faggot!

Some young men howled at him
ran in a pack
reverted to some ancient form
they took Claude
took his money
yelled faggot
as they cast his body
in front of a car.

III

How many cars have you dodged Berri?
How many ancient young men have you met?
Perhaps your size saved you
but then you were not always this size
perhaps your fleetness
perhaps
there are no more ancient young men.

Ah!   Within this lifestyle
we have chosen.
Sing?
What do you mean
you wanna be a singer?
Best get a good government job
maybe sing on the side.
You heard the words:
Be responsible
Be respectable
Be stable
Be secure
Be normal, boy.

How many quarter-filled rooms
have you sang your soul to
then washed away with
blended whiskey?

I told my booking agent one year
book me a tour
Blackberri and I
will travel this land
together
take our Black Queerness
into the face
of this place and say

Hey, here we are
a faggot & a dyke, Black
we make good music
& write good poems
We Be—Something Else.

My agent couldn't book us.
It seemed my lesbian audiences
were not ready for my faggot
brother
and I remembered
a law conference
in San Francisco
where women
women who loved women
threw boos and tomatoes
at a woman who dared
to have a man in her band.

What is this world we have?
Is my house the only safe place
for us?
And I am rage
all the low-paying gigs
all the uncut records
all the dodged cars
all the fear escaping
all the unclaimed love
so I offer my bosom
and food
and shudder
fearful of the time
when it will not be
enough
fearful of the time
when the ritual
ends.

georgia, georgia
georgia on my mind

I

It came at first
like a rumor
traveling through
Black pages
of *Jet* and *Ebony*
children are missing
children are dead
in a southern metropolis
the common denominator
Black and young.

It comes again
now a nasty gnawing truth
Black bodies float up
from rivers and ditches
each week
more missing
more dead.

II

Now let the circus begin.
Proper politicians
come to town
reporters run from
family to family
look and see
the crying mother
at her child's funeral
look and see
the scared commissioners
'We're doing all we can.'

III

Fear raises its head
the unspoken belief
the killers
white,
the Klan, the Nazis
maniacs, crazies
genocide
eliminate the young
stop the breeding
Black friends angry
bitter scream
'those lousy bastards'
'those racist fiends'
white friends afraid
better to be quiet
and hope it's one insane fool.

IV

The lessons are
slowly slipped out
it's a shame *but*
if the kids were
not in the streets
Mother
why weren't you home
with your child?
the President says
he'll send more money for
investigation
two weeks after he
announced his budget cuts
the police psychologist
swears the killers
are Black
'the kids wouldn't trust
a white'
and half the nation prays
he's right.

My anger rises
I know who the killers are
and know the killer will go untried
see no court or judges
no jury of peers
the killers wear the suits of
businessmen
buy ghetto apartments
and overcharge the rent
the killers lock Black men
in prison or drive
them from their homes
the killers give the Black woman
a job
and pay her one-half of what she
needs to live
the killers scream about
juvenile crime
and refuse to build childcare centers.
It won't matter what
demented fool is caught
for society has provided
the lure.

A rich kid is not tempted
by candy
a rich kid is not tempted
by movies
a rich kid is not tempted
by attention.
Long after the murders of
Atlanta are solved
the killer will remain free.

one thanksgiving day

One Thanksgiving Day
Priscilla Ford
got into her
Lincoln Continental
drove to Virginia Street
in downtown Reno
and ran over thirty people.
Six of them died.

One Thanksgiving Day
Priscilla Ford
got into her
Lincoln Continental
drove to Virginia Street
in downtown Reno
and ran over thirty people.
Six of them died.

Priscilla, Priscilla
who did you see?
what face from your past?
Was it the waitress
who waited to wait
on you?
Was it the clerk
who tried to sell you
only the
brightest colored clothes?
Was it your child's
teacher who tried to
teach her that she was
slow?
Was it the security guard
at the bank who guarded
you from the bank's money
with his eyes?
One Thanksgiving Day
Priscilla Ford
got into her
Lincoln Continental
drove to Virginia Street
in downtown Reno
and ran over thirty people.
Six of them died.

Screams filled the street
panic ran through the crowd
like a losing streak
at the blackjack tables
and the state of Nevada
was stunned.
A tired middle-aged Black woman
was not thankful that day
not thankful for her job
wrapping gifts at Macy's
not thankful for the state
taking custody of her child
she was not thankful
for her Lincoln Continental.

Priscilla Ford
got into her Lincoln Continental
and hurled through the streets of Reno
the killer made in Motown factories
swept down on tourists
looking to make a big hit
hit by a navy blue
steel bludgeon
screams dying beneath its wheels
and the state of Nevada
was angry.

She went to trial.
Insanity
her lawyers pled
she was crazy with anger
she was crazy with fear
she was crazy with defeat
she was crazy with isolation
no sane person kills
strangers with their cars
Priscilla Ford said yes
I drove my car
into the whiteness
of Nevada streets
she would say nothing more
and the state of Nevada
was frightened.
If Priscilla Ford could do it
who else?
How many Black faces
that emptied garbage
waited tables
bagged groceries
wrapped presents
were capable?

Reaction was swift.
One entrepreneur
printed a card
it said *Happy Thanksgiving*
with a picture of Priscilla
on its front
inside it said
Sorry I Missed YOU.

Priscilla Ford
got into her
Lincoln Continental
drove to Virginia Street
in downtown Reno
and ran over thirty people.
Six of them died
and the state of Nevada
was vindictive.
You cannot be insane
to be enraged is not insane
to be filled with hatred is not insane
to lash out at whiteness is not insane
it is being a nigger
it is your place in life.

Priscilla Ford
got into her
Lincoln Continental
drove to Virginia Street
in downtown Reno
and ran over thirty people.
Six of them died
and now Priscilla Ford
will die.
The state of Nevada
has judged

that it is
not crazy
for Black folks
to kill white folks
with their cars.

Priscilla Ford
will be
the second woman
executed in Nevada's history.
It's her highest
finish in life.

aftermath

for Marty

Did you know I watch you
as you cuddle with sleep?
Propped on my elbow,
close, your breath brushes
back silence
like a swimmer parting water.
Your lips are tight
now.
If I close my eyes
they become a cool drink
full and wet
house an active tongue
that travels my body
like an explorer
retracing familiar ground.

If I close my eyes
I can feel your tongue
dart
from my ear
to my neck
to the crevice
a prospector
pause to take samples
inspect the ore
then move on.

If I close my eyes
I can feel your tongue
wrap around my nipples
tuck them
deep
in the corner
of your mouth
and suck them
suck them
parched flowers.

If I close my eyes
oh love
if I close my eyes
I become once again
your hopeless captive
ready to submit.

I think of the
straight person who
asks what do you
do in bed?
Oh
how many times
have I
asked the same thing.

breaking up

You'd think after spending
two years with a woman
you'd know her
you'd know what she likes to eat
and when
what she likes to wear
how she likes her hair
you'd know her favorite colors
her favorite TV shows
her favorite author
and so much more
you'd know when she's pre-menstrual
you'd know when she's uptight
you'd know when she's angry
and when she wants to fight
but then
you break up
she never liked the color blue
she never liked your gumbo
your snoring drove her crazy
she can't stand bar-be-que
she doesn't like the way you drive
she doesn't like your friends
she hates the way you comb your hair
she doesn't like her steak cooked rare
she doesn't like your politics
or anything you do

the truth it seems
in this time and place
is she really can't stand you.

You'd think after spending
two years with a woman
you'd know her
but it seems that love
like everything else
is relative.

maybe i should have been a teacher

The next person who asks
'Have you written anything new?'
just might get hit
or at least snarled at
or cursed out.
I got a week's vacation
from work
the first
in at least two years.
The first day of vacation
I cleaned my house
scrubbed walls and floors
prepared it and me
to write.
The second day of vacation
I bought two reams of paper
a new ribbon for my typewriter
groceries to last the week.
The third day of vacation
the dog comes home
from his nocturnal run
he doesn't eat
his nose is dry
off to the vet
parvovirus

he'll die, no doubt,
but I doubt
been my dog
for twelve years
and I'm not ready
for him to die
so antibiotics
and broth every
two hours
and maybe he'll live.
Pick up the kid
teacher says
'she's been quiet today'
my kid is many things
at different times
what she's not
is quiet
take the kid home
temperature 100 degrees
call Alicia
'What do you do
for fever?'
aspirins, liquids,
no drafts.

So the routine begins.
Give the dog
his medicine
give the kid
her medicine
try and get
his stool for the vet
try and get
her to stay in bed
three days later
the dog is fine
the kid is fine
I'm exhausted
and it's time to
go back to work.
At work
start work on
the new protocols*
go to directors' meeting
write a speech for a rally
on the weekend
lab work returns
no products of conception
call the woman
get a sonogram
she's pregnant—but
in her stomach

*guidelines used by health care
practitioners for patient exams.

somebody forgot
to turn on the alarm
that we got
after being ripped
off four times
letter comes from
the IRS
I'm being audited
for 1978
they want more money
a friend calls
she's broken up
with her lover
and is afraid to get
her clothes
could I please
go with her?
she doesn't want
to call the police
I decide to go
to the bar and drink
woman decides
I'm flirting with
the bartender
who she's been
flirting with
all night

now I'm in a fight
now I'm in another fight
outside the bar
and cop cars are
coming from everywhere
and I remember
my mother telling me
I should be a teacher
and me saying
but I want to write
paint pictures
with words
read poems for people
and I get a call
from a sister
who wants me
to come read
for her college
but they only have
money for advertising

and I see me
giving Ma Bell
a poster
for my January phone bill
which is huge
since I called
my friend in New York
to say I think
I'm going mad here
cause my lover
who isn't my lover
because we haven't
defined the relationship
as such
thinks we're getting
too close
seen each other
five days in a row
after the fight
we had two weeks ago
because
I had not shown
enough caring
or commitment

decides maybe
we should be
good friends
who fuck
at least
we do
that very well
and why deprive
our bodies
even if we can't
get our heads
in synch
and I think
maybe
the next person
who asks
'Have you
written anything
new?'
just might get hit.

child's play

Have you ever
tried to explain
human behavior
to a four-year old?
Spend the first years
saying learn to share
daughter
being selfish
self-centered
is not worthwhile
let Jamie play
with your toys
and Susie and Leotis as well.
Then Leotis decides
he should have
the pinball machine
not you
takes it away
to wherever he lives
and four-year-old tears
are asking
why
isn't Leotis sharing
my toy with me?

I want to scream
at Leotis for making
my task harder
and it doesn't matter
then
that Leotis is poor
so are we
and it doesn't matter
that
Leotis has four
brothers and sisters
I want to kill
Leotis' mother
don't understand
her
accepting toys
she didn't buy
but I can't tell
this four-year old
with tears wanting
to know why
her toy is gone
any of my anger

I calculate
the pinball machine
cost eight dollars
and pay day
is ten days away
and if I write a check
and it takes two days
to get to their bank
and then two days
to get to mine
it still has
six days to bounce.
But should I
just replace it?
There's a lesson here—
be careful of your toys
but the earlier lesson
of sharing
didn't
say *with caution*
and so I offer
a trip to the park
it's free and a diversion
and we can swing
and play on slides
and she says yes
let's go to the park.

I am angered
even more because
I know Leotis
didn't take
just a toy
he took away
some of my child's
childness.

jonestown

As a child in Texas
race education
was simple
was subtle
was sharp

The great lone star
state sharply
placed me
in colored schools
with colored teachers
and colored books
and colored knowledge

I shopped in white stores
and bought colored clothes
'Keep the colors loud and bright
so they dazzle in the night
No matter where a nigger's bred
they love yellow, orange and red'

I used colored toilets
and rode colored buses home
I went to colored churches
with colored preachers
and prayed to a white God
begged forgiveness for Cain
and his sins
and his descendants
us lowly colored sinners
and the message
was simple
was sharp
there is a place for niggers
but not among good white folk

At home
race education
was simple
was subtle
fact gleaned
by differences

The white man
who jumped
free-fall
in the sky
was quietly dismissed
'white folks are crazy'
the white man
who turned
somersaults
on Sports Spectacular skis
was quietly dismissed
'white folks will do anything
for money'
the white man who
shot and killed his wife
and children
and then himself
received a headshake
and a sigh
and the simple statement
'white folks are crazy'

And the messages
fell into place
white folks went crazy
and went to nut houses
Black folks got mad
and went to jail
white folks started wars
Black folks died in them
white folks owned America
Black folks built it

As I grew into adulthood
many messages were discarded
many were forgotten
but one returns to haunt me

Black folks do not commit suicide
Black folks do not
Black folks do not
Black folks do not commit suicide

November 18, 1978
more than 900 people
most of them Black
died in a man-made town
called Jonestown

Newscasters' words
slap me in my face
peoples' tears and grief
emanate from my set
and I remember the lessons
rehear a childhood message

Black folks do not commit suicide

I thought of my uncle Dave
he died in prison
suicide
the authorities said
'Boy just up and hung hisself'
and I remember my mother
her disbelief, her grief
'Them white folks kilt my brother
Dave didn't commit no suicide'
and the funeral
a bitter quiet funeral
his coffin sealed from sighters
and we all knew
Dave died not by his hands
some guard decided
that nigger should die

And I stare at the newscaster
he struggles to contain himself
it's a BIG BIG story
and he must not
seem too excited

'American troops made a
grizzly discovery today
in Jonestown, Guyana'
my innards scream as
the facts unfold
'a communist preacher'
and I see old Black women
my grandmothers
communist   NO
little old Black ladies
do not believe in communists
they believe in God
and Jesus   yet,
the newscasters' words
a *commune*
a media storm of
words and pictures
interviews with ex-members
survivors, city officials

the *San Francisco Chronicle*
had a problem with its presses
erratic delivery
of the morning paper
and in two days the *Chronicle*
publishes a book
Eyewitness Account
by a staff reporter
who survived
the airport attack
and the story grows
STEP RIGHT UP
STEP RIGHT UP
Ladies and Gentlemen
have I got a tale
for you
we got these men
two men
a congressman & a preacher
& a supporting cast of hundreds
the congressman went
to investigate the preacher
and wound up dead
the preacher wound up dead
the supporting cast
wound up dead
and all the dead
are singing to me

Black folks do not
Black folks do not
Black folks do not commit suicide

My phone rings
newscaster mistakenly says
Patricia *Parker*
not *Parks*
died on the airstrip
a friend
wants to know
are you alive?

Yes
I am here
not there
festering
in a jungle
with bloated belly
not a victim
in a dream deferred
not a piece
in a media puzzle
not a member
in the supporting cast.

Yet
I am there
walking with the souls
of Black folks
crying
screaming
WHY   WHY
Black folks
why are you here
and dead?
tell me how you
willingly died
did the minister
sing to you
'Kool-aid Kool-aid
taste great
I like Kool-aid
can't wait'

I see Black people
beautiful Black people
in lines in front of a tub
of twentieth-century hemlock
I see guards with guns
guns   guns
why guns?

and the pictures
continue to flow
images of a man
a church man
he cures disease
NO
he's a fake
hired people
treated liver
he loves God
NO
he's a communist
he talks many messages
revolution to the young
God to the old
he believes in the family
NO
he destroys the family
fucks the women
fucks the men
and the media continues
to tell the tale

•

An interview with a live one.
'You were a member of People's Temple?'
'Yes, I was.'
'Why did you join?'
'Well, I went there a few times
and then I stopped going, but
the Rev. Jones came by my house
and asked me why I quit coming.
I was really surprised.
No one had ever cared
that much about me before.'

No one had ever cared
that much about me before
and it came home
the messages of my youth
came clear
the Black people
in Jonestown
did not commit suicide
they were murdered
they were murdered in
small southern towns
they were murdered in
big northern cities

they were murdered
as school children
by teachers
who didn't care
they were murdered
by policemen
who didn't care
they were murdered
by welfare workers
who didn't care
they were murdered
by shopkeepers
who didn't care
they were murdered
by church people
who didn't care
they were murdered
by politicians
who didn't care
they didn't die at Jonestown
they went to Jonestown dead
convinced that America
and Americans
didn't care

they died
in the schoolrooms
they died
in the streets
they died
in the bars
they died
in the jails
they died
in the churches
they died
in the welfare lines

Jim Jones was not the cause
he was the result
of 400 years
of not caring

Black folks do not
Black folks do not
Black folks do not commit suicide

legacy

for Anastasia Jean

'Anything handed down
from, or as from an
ancestor to a descendant.'

Prologue

There are those who think
or perhaps don't think
that children and lesbians
together can't make a family
that we create an extension
of perversion.

They think
or perhaps don't think
that we have different relationships
with our children
that instead of getting up
in the middle of the night
for a 2 AM and 6 AM feeding
we rise up and chant
'you're gonna be a dyke
you're gonna be a dyke.'

That we feed our children
lavender Similac
and by breathing our air
the chilren's genitals distort
and they become hermaphrodites.

They ask
'What will you say to them
what will you teach them?'

Child
that would be mine
I bring you my world
and bid it be yours.

I
Addie and George

He was a small man
son of an African slave
his father came chained
in a boat
long after the boats
had 'stopped' coming
his skin was ebony
shone like new piano keys.

He was a carpenter
worked long in the trade
of the christ he chose
six days a week
his hands plied the wood
gave birth to houses
and cabinets and tables
on the seventh day
he lay down his hammer
and picked up his bible
and preached the gospel
to his brethren
led his flock in prayer

when he was seventy-nine years old
he lay down
in the presence of his wife
and children
and died.

Her father too was a slave
common law wed to an indian squaw
Addie came colored caramel
long black hair
high cheek bones.

She was a christian woman
her religion a daily occurrence
her allegiance was to God,
her husband, her children
in that order
together she and George
had twenty-two children
many never survived
the first year of life
a fact not unusual
for the time.

When she was seventy-six
George died
she began to travel
to the homes of her children
to make sure they led
a christian life
the children hid
their beer and bourbon
the grandchildren hid
she would come for two months
then move on
leave the words of Jehovah
sweating from the walls
when she was ninety-four years old
she lay down
and died.

II
Ernest and Marie

He came from the earth, they say,
an expression meaning *orphan*
parents in the hands of poverty
best give the boy away
and so he came to live
in a good christian home
with a good christian minister
and his wife
he was a man of many trades
roofer in the summer
tire retreader in the winter
earned far beyond
his four years of education
he wanted to see
all of his children
get educated
he lived long enough to see
his children gone and grown
and then
he lay down
and died.

She was the youngest of the twenty-two
quiet woman
tall for her time
she bore eight children
five survived the early years
she raised them in a christian way
by day she cleaned houses
by night she cleaned her own
she was sixty-two when her husband died
took her first plane trip that same year
when her third daughter was killed
she cremated her child and went home
willed herself sick and weary
she took three years to complete the task
then she lay down
and died.

III

It is from this past that I come
surrounded by sisters in blood
and in spirit
it is this past
that I bequeath
a history of work and struggle.

Each generation improves the world
for the next.
My grandparents willed me strength.
My parents willed me pride.
I will to you rage.
I give you a world incomplete
a world
where
women still
are property and chattel
where
color still
shuts doors
where
sexual choice still
threatens
but I give you
a legacy
of doers
of people who take risks
to chisel the crack wider.

Take the strength that you may
wage a long battle.
Take the pride that you can
never stand small.
Take the rage that you can
never settle for less.

These be the things I pass
to you my daughter
if this is the result of perversion
let the world stand screaming.
You will mute their voices
with your life.

Other titles from Firebrand Books include:

Mohawk Trail by Beth Brant
Moll Cutpurse, a Novel by Ellen Galford